Profiles in Greek and Roman Mythology

HADES

Mitchell Lane
PUBLISHERS
P.O. Box 196
Hockessin, Delaware 19707
Visit us on the web: www.mitchelllane.com
Comments? email us: mitchelllane@mitchelllane.com

PROFILES IN GREEK AND ROMAN MYTHOLOGY

Titles in the Series

Achilles
Apollo
Artemis
Athena
Dionysus
Hades
Hephaestus
Hercules
Hermes
Jason
Odysseus
Perseus
Poseidon
Theseus
Zeus

Profiles in Greek and Roman Mythology

HADES

Kayleen Reusser

Mitchell Lane

PUBLISHERS
P.O. Box 196
Hockessin, Delaware 19707
Visit us on the web: www.mitchelllane.com
Comments? email us: mitchelllane@mitchelllane.com

Mitchell Lane
PUBLISHERS

Printing   1   2   3   4   5   6   7   8   9

Library of Congress Cataloging-in-Publication Data
Reusser, Kayleen.
  Hades / by Kayleen Reusser.
      p. cm. — (Profiles in Greek and Roman mythology)
  Includes bibliographical references and index.
  ISBN 978-1-58415-750-2 (library bound)
  1. Hades (Greek deity)—Juvenile literature. I. Title.
  BL820.P58R48 2010
  398.20938'01—dc22
                                                                    2009045663

ABOUT THE AUTHOR: Kayleen Reusser is a freelance writer who lives in Bluffton, Indiana. She has published hundreds of articles for books, including *Chicken Soup for the Soul,* magazines, and newspapers. Reusser has written other books for Mitchell Lane, including *Taylor Swift, Selena Gomez, Hephaestus,* and *Hermes.* Find out more about her at www.KayleenR.com.

AUTHOR'S NOTE: The stories retold in this book use dialog as an aid to readability. The dialog is based on the author's research.

PUBLISHER'S NOTE: This story is based on the author's extensive research, which she believes to be accurate. Documentation of such research is on page 46.
   The internet sites referenced herein were active as of the publication date. Due to the fleeting nature of some web sites, we cannot guarantee they will all be active when you are reading this book.
   To reflect current usage, we have chosen to use the secular era designations BCE ("before the common era") and CE ("of the common era") instead of the traditional designations BC ("before Christ") and AD (*anno Domini,* "in the year of the Lord").

TABLE OF CONTENTS

Profiles in Greek and Roman Mythology

Hades, the god of the Underworld, relied on Cerberus, his three-headed hound, to guard the gate between the living and the dead. Some myths say that Cerberus had fifty heads.

HADES

One night, long after the fires in the Titan camp had burned to embers, Hades (HAY-deez) crept among the sleeping soldiers. Careful not to disturb the bodies stretched on the ground, he watched for signs of movement. All appeared still. The only sounds were snores from the soldiers.

A few feet away, a soldier mumbled in his sleep. Hades laughed quietly. It wouldn't matter if all of the soldiers in the camp opened their eyes and looked straight at him. Hades wore the helmet that made him invisible.

Hurriedly, he snatched up the enemy's weapons. At the camp on the other side of the hill, Hades dumped the swords and shields at the feet of his brother, Zeus (ZOOS). "Now the ten-year war can end," he told Zeus. "The Titans will have nothing with which to fight us."

It had begun when the goddess Rhea and god Cronos (KROH-nus) became parents to Hades and his five brothers and sisters. The children were called Olympians because they lived on Mount Olympus in Greece. (Later, more gods would join them.)

Rhea loved her children, but Cronos feared them. He believed in the curse from his father—that one of Cronos' children would kill him. Cronos wanted to live, so he swallowed his five children as they were born. Hades was one of them.

Horrified at this act, Rhea cried for her lost children. She wanted another baby, but knew her husband would not allow it to live.

Rhea thought for a long time about what to do. Finally, she developed a plan. The next time she became pregnant, she went to a cave in the land of Crete. After she delivered the baby, Cronos came to

see her. Rhea handed him something wrapped in a blanket. Believing it to be the baby, he swallowed the whole thing without looking inside. When he left, Rhea reached into a corner of the cave where she had laid her baby, whom she named Zeus. Cronos had swallowed a rock inside the blanket.

Zeus grew up without Cronos' knowledge on the island of Crete near Greece. Rhea still wanted to free her five other children from Cronos' belly. She waited several years, then she said to Cronos, "My lord, you should find a young cupbearer to assist you. All of the great kings have cupbearers to fill their chalices with drink."

When Cronos agreed, Rhea presented Zeus to him. "This mortal from Crete will assist you, my king," she said. The king didn't recognize his son, who had grown into a strong young man.

Rhea and Zeus knew the ruse was risky. If Cronos discovered Zeus was his son, Cronos would destroy him.

Zeus and Rhea mixed a special drink for Cronos made of mustard, salt, and nectar. Cronos drank it all and asked for more. Zeus refilled his master's cup.

The recipe had a strange effect on Cronos. He began to twitch and gasp. Then he vomited, spewing forth the stone he had swallowed years before. Hades and his siblings—Poseidon (poh-SY-dun), Hestia (HES-tee-uh), Hera (HAYR-uh), and Demeter (DIH-mih-ter)—also came up, alive and whole.

Cronos was not happy about being tricked. He remembered the curse and persuaded his brothers and sisters, the gigantic Titans, to fight his own children. The war lasted ten years. Sometimes the Titans seemed to be winning. Other times, Zeus' army appeared to be on top.

Zeus freed the Cyclopes (sy-KLOH-peez) and the Hundred-Handed Ones, who had been held prisoner by Cronos in a remote part of the Underworld called Tartarus (TAR-tur-us). These monsters helped the children of Cronos fight against the Titans. The Cyclopes, who were huge and had only one eye in the middle of their fore-

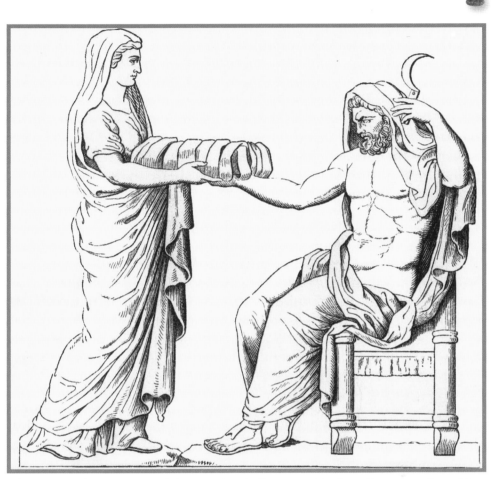

When the goddess Rhea handed her husband, Cronos, a blanket, Cronos swallowed it. He thought he had disposed of his son Zeus. Instead, Rhea had tricked the god by wrapping the blanket around a rock.

heads, were strong and skilled craftsmen. They forged special weapons to use in the war. Hades received the helmet that made him invisible. Poseidon was given a trident—a spear with three prongs. For Zeus they designed a powerful thunderbolt.

With his new weapon, Hades sneaked in to the Titan camp to discover how many soldiers were there and to take their weapons.

When he returned, a great cheer arose from the Cyclopes, the Hundred-Handed Ones, and the rest of Zeus' army. They congratulated Hades on his bravery.

According to the Greek myth on which this story is based, when the Titans woke up and realized their weapons were gone, they still marched into battle.[1]

Cronos realized his army was no match for Zeus' soldiers. Reluctantly, he surrendered. Zeus banished them to Tartarus. There, behind a sturdy bronze fence, the Titans were guarded for eternity.

After the war ended, Hades, Zeus, and their siblings ruled Earth and its upper and lower regions. They divided the world into kingdoms. Poseidon ruled the sea and gained the power to create earthquakes. Zeus was made ruler of the sky, mountains, and land. Demeter became the goddess of grains and other growing things. Hestia, the kindest and sweetest among the gods, chose the hearth as her kingdom. And Hera, the wife of Zeus, became the protector of home and marriage. Nothing was left for Hades but the Underworld, where souls went after death. Hades eagerly took control of his new kingdom.[2]

In ancient times, the Greeks believed the earth was flat. They placed the Underworld in the Far West, which they thought was empty of people and animals and plants. As adventurers traveled to lands far west beyond the Mediterranean Sea, they discovered people living there. The Greeks decided the Underworld was a region under the earth. They called the place the same name as its ruler: Hades.

Many ancient writers contributed to the story about the Underworld's appearance. All agreed that it was not a pleasant place. According to Dante Alighieri, who described the Underworld and the unfortunate souls who dwelled there in his classic epic poem *Inferno,* it was a "low place where a thick pitch boiled and bubbled."[3] Hesiod described it as "a murky earth" and that "even the gods abhor it for it's dank and horrid there. A monstrous yawning

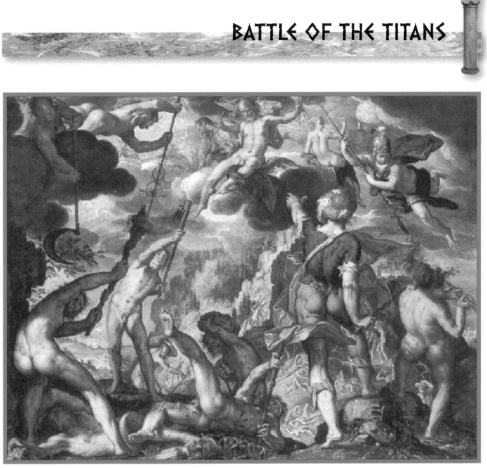

The Battle Between the Gods and the Titans by Dutch painter Joachim Wtewael. The war became known as the Titanomachy.

chasm . . . in the circling of a year no man would reach its bottom."[4]

Though he was the king of the Underworld, Hades was not liked or admired as a god. His name inspired great fear, and people never spoke of him without trembling. No temples were dedicated to Hades, and statues of him are rare.[5]

Yet even though the stories the Greeks created about Hades made him appear as a grim figure, he was not considered an evil god. He did not bring death—that was the job of Thanatos (THAN-uh-tohs). Neither did he torment his inmates—the task of punishing wrongdoers was left to the Furies.[6]

The Greeks believed the rest of the gods lived on Mount Olympus, located on today's maps in a region of eastern Greece called Thessaly (THEH-suh-lee). Mount Olympus rises to a height of 9,570 feet (2,919 meters); it is the highest peak in Greece. No winds, rain, or snow ever entered the gods' heavenly kingdom.

On Mount Olympus, dozens of gods and goddesses feasted on ambrosia (am-BROH-zjuh) and nectar and listened to sweet music. (No one knows for sure what ingredients were in ambrosia, the food and drink of the gods, but it may have contained a mixture of honey, water, fruit, olive oil, cheese, and barley. Eating it could make a mortal immortal. Nectar, a drink usually served with ambrosia, may have been made by fermenting honey.[7])

While the atmosphere in Olympus was generally happy, the opposite was true in the Underworld. It was dark and gloomy and generally a frustrating place for its inhabitants. Although we don't know much about the food or eating habits of the souls in Hades, two stories illustrate unfulfillment on those subjects. As punishment for his actions, Tantalus suffered perpetual hunger and thirst. Another tale says that when Persephone ate a pomegranate seed, she was doomed to an unhappy marriage.[8]

Hades didn't care if mortals feared him as the god of the afterlife, or that the other gods lived far away on Mount Olympus. The area beneath the Earth was thought to contain precious gems and rare metals, such as emeralds, diamonds, gold, and silver. As ruler of the Underworld, Hades was rich. [9]

Still, the souls that entered Hades were not thrilled to be there. Each one had the same question as it approached the entrance to the Underworld: Will I be rewarded or punished in Hades? Not even the gods knew the answer, which would count for eternity.

Pluto—Roman God of the Underworld

Just as the Greeks made up stories to explain events and oddities they didn't understand, so did the Romans. When they conquered Greece, the Romans adopted the Greek stories, changing only a few details. Hades was the Greek name of the place where souls went after death and the god who ruled there. The Roman people referred to the god of the Lower World and his kingdom as Pluto.[10]

Pluto and Hades shared similar characteristics. Each of their domains contained Tartarus. This chamber had the dubious distinction of being at the bottom of the Underworld while functioning as a place of eternal pain. In his book *Dialogues of the Dead,* Baron George Lyttelton Lyttelton describes it this way: "We will throw them down to the bottom of Tartarus in spite of Pluto and all his guards."[11]

Pluto and Proserpina

The gods of the Roman and Greek Underworlds were married to females with similar names—Pluto's bride was Proserpina; Hades' bride was Persephone.

Originally Dis was the name the Romans gave to Pluto. *Dis* was taken from the Latin word *dives,* which means "rich."[12]

Dante applies the name Dis to Lucifer and to the city at the base of the Underworld (Hell), where Lucifer is forever stationed. The walls of the city of Dis mark the division between upper and lower Hell. In the upper are five of the Seven Deadly Sins—lust, gluttony, avarice, sloth, and wrath. The lower seems to contain what Dante considers the more evil sins—Envy and Pride.[13]

If you've heard someone say "By Jove," you've heard a less-than-pleasant reference to Pluto. Jupiter was the Roman equivalent of Zeus, the greatest Greek god. "Jove" became a nickname for Jupiter. Eventually it came to be part of a curse that referred to Pluto, the place of death.

Arrival of Charon, by Gustave Doré, illustrated the 1857 edition of Dante's Inferno. Dante combined classical mythology with Christian beliefs when he wrote *Divine Comedy* in the early 1300s. The first part of the work, *The Inferno,* focuses on the Underworld.

HADES

CHAPTER 2

Hades' Hospitality

Hades established a strict procedure for admittance to his kingdom. Only the souls of the dead were allowed entrance. Hades did not even allow other gods to enter his home—with one exception. The god Hermes (HUR-meez), a son of Zeus, became the messenger of the gods. One of his tasks was to usher each soul down from the Land of the Living to the River Styx, the boundary of the Underworld. There they would meet an old man named Charon (KAYR-on), who ferried the souls across the river's cool, sluggish waters. In *The Inferno,* Dante describes the scene:

> A veteran who with ancient hair was white
> Shouting: "Ye souls depraved, be filled with fear.
> Hope never more of Heaven to win the sight;
> I come to take you to the other strand [shore],
> To frost and fire and everlasting night.
> And thou, O living soul, who there dost stand,
> From 'mong the dead withdraw thee."[1]

The Greeks believed Charon expected each soul to pay for passage into Hades. Thus a coin called an obol was placed beneath the tongue of each dead person before burial.[2]

Each time Charon took his boat across the Styx, corpses of those who had not received a proper burial on Earth and therefore had no coin to pay raised their rotting hands, pleading to be hauled into the boat. Charon

Obol

would only receive into his boat the souls of those who carried their passage money and who had been properly buried.[3]

Styx, also known as the River of Hate, was so sacred, the gods swore binding oaths by it. It was not the only river in Hades, though it is the most well known. Other rivers in Hades included the Cocytus (Lamentation or Wailing), Phlegethon (Fire), and Lethe (Forgetfulness). The Acheron was known as the River of Sadness or Woe.[4]

Lethe probably was so named because one tradition said that a sip from this river erased every memory of life on earth from a soul's mind. John Milton wrote in *Paradise Lost,* "Lethe, the river of oblivion, rolls/Her watery labyrinth, whereof who drinks,/Forthwith his former state and being forgets—/Forgets both joy and grief, pleasure and pain."[5]

In this 19th-century painting of Charon ferrying souls across the River Styx, Ukrainian artist Olexandr Lytovchenko includes the figures of Virgil and Dante looking on (background, right).

In general, spirits in Hades didn't talk of families or ones left behind, because on the boat journey with Charon, each soul drank from the River Lethe. However, in some of the Greek myths, such as those describing Aeneas' and Achilles' visits to the Underworld, some souls did recall their lifetime experiences while in Hades.

Souls who made it across the Styx met another obstacle at the gates to Hades—the fearsome watchdog Cerberus (SER-ber-us, or KER-ber-us). According to Hesiod, it was an "impossible, unspeakable cur of Hades, fifty-headed with great power. Shameless, he had a brazen voice and raw flesh would devour."[6]

Hesiod adds even more description of this hideous beast: "Keeping watch outside them is a dreadful, ruthless hound:/with wicked skill he fawns on every victim that appears—/He wags his tail for all of them and perks up both his ears; /but none he lets go out again—he watches at all hours—/and anyone who tries to leave he seizes and devours."[7]

Once a soul made it past Cerberus, it found Hades' kingdom crowded and busy. Inside the gates, the king of the Underworld sat on his throne. Near the throne sat three judges: Minos (MY-nohs), Rhadamanthys (rad-uh-MAN-this), and Aeacus (EE-uh-kus). They questioned all the new souls and sorted each one's good and bad thoughts and actions. Depending on what they discovered about a soul's past life on earth, the judges decided where the soul would spend eternity.[8]

If a person had been extremely evil while alive, or if the person had angered the gods, his or her soul was sent to the dreaded section of the Underworld called Tartarus, where the gates were iron and the floor bronze. Tartarus was the deepest pit under the earth, as far beneath Hades as Heaven is above the earth.[9]

And although it was a place, Tartarus was also the father of the monsters Typhon and Echidna.[10] Typhon was defeated by Zeus, who pinned him under Mount Etna during the Titanomachy.[11]

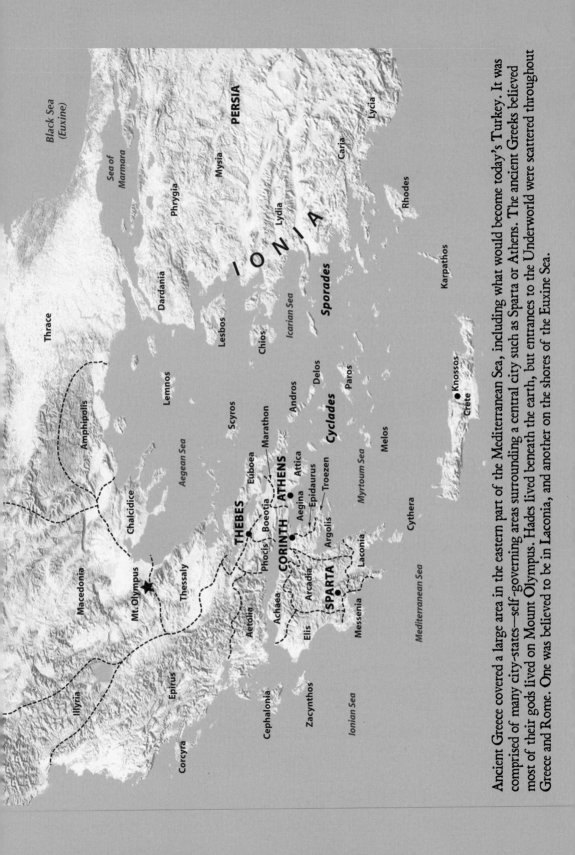

Ancient Greece covered a large area in the eastern part of the Mediterranean Sea, including what would become today's Turkey. It was comprised of many city-states—self-governing areas surrounding a central city such as Sparta or Athens. The ancient Greeks believed most of their gods lived on Mount Olympus. Hades lived beneath the earth, but entrances to the Underworld were scattered throughout Greece and Rome. One was believed to be in Laconia, and another on the shores of the Euxine Sea.

Tartarus was a gloomy, dark prison with special guards called the Hundred-Handers. Hesiod refers to these three huge, mighty beasts—known as Kottos, Briareos, and Gyges—as "monstrous forms with 100 arms. From each sturdy shoulder sprouted 50 heads."[12]

Many guilty souls in Tartarus had to face the Furies, or Erinyes (er-IN-yeez). Their name means "the angry ones." These three immortal women—Alecto, Tisiphone, and Megaera—were often sent to earth to punish living people who behaved cruelly to family members.[13] Some Greek myths said the Furies could pass the sun in its orbit in their eagerness to dole out their punishments.[14] In Aeschylus' play *Eumenides,* they are depicted as disgusting, loathsome creatures dressed in black and wreathed in snakes.[15]

When not hounding the guilty on earth, the Furies pestered wrongdoers in the Underworld. Some of the most famous of these criminals were the fifty Danaids. These beautiful daughters of Danaus had fifty cousins—sons of Aegyptus—who wanted to marry them. Danaus believed that his brother Aegyptus only wanted their children to marry so that Aegyptus would rule Danaus' land as well as his own. Danaus fled with his daughters, but in the end, he was forced to agree to the marriages. Wanting to protect his daughters, he gave each a dagger, with instructions to kill her bridegroom on their wedding night.

All of the daughters, except one, obeyed their father. Since the girls had killed their husbands, the Furies sentenced them to eternal punishment: They had to fetch water from the River Styx to fill Hades' garden pond. The problem was the jars had holes at the bottom like sieves, so the girls could never finish their task. They trudged endlessly and eternally back and forth between the pond and the river.

One daughter, Hypermestra, did not kill her bridegroom, because she had fallen in love with him. He became king after Danaus died. The gods rewarded Hypermestra by sending her to the Elysian (ee-LEE-zhun) Fields when she died.[16]

The Danaides, by John William Waterhouse (1903), depicts the eternal punishment of the Danaids.

The Elysian Fields (also called Elysium) were the realm of Hades for the souls of those who had been good in life more often than bad. In *The Odyssey*, Homer writes this about the Elysian Fields: "where life glides on in immortal ease for mortal man; no snow, no winter, never a downpour but night and day the Ocean River sends up breezes, singing winds of the West refreshing all mankind.[17]

The poet Hesiod pictures the inhabitants of the Elysian Fields as farmers who look forward to a productive harvest: "Three times a year the fertile earth grows ripe and is increased, and happy are the heroes to whom it bears delightful grain."[18]

Hades ruled his crowded, busy kingdom well. Outside Elysium, most of the souls could not recall being happy. Except for the souls in Tartarus, they were not sad, either.

Still, Hades realized his kingdom was not complete. He wanted a queen to sit beside him. He thought long and hard about whom his empress should be. Hades had few friends, and none of them volunteered to help him. Finally, he went to Zeus for advice. Zeus had just the right person in mind. Unfortunately, his choice would cause misery over the entire Earth.

The Furies and Orestes

The Furies play a big part in a trilogy of plays known as the *Oresteia*, written by Aeschylus around 458 BCE. In the opening scene of the third play, called *Eumenides*, a priestess crawls onstage. Appalled by the hideous sight of the Furies, she is unable to stand. She describes them this way: "But for blackness they are loathsome and their apparel is not fit . . . the breed of these visitors I have never seen, nor know any land which boasts to raise this kind and not to suffer for it and repent the pains."[19]

In the first play of the trilogy, *Agamemnon*, the Greek king of Argos, Agamemnon (aa-guh-MEM-non), has just returned victorious from the Trojan War. Before he left for Troy, he sacrificed his daughter, Iphigenia (ih-fih-jih-NY-uh), so that the gods might grant him strong winds to swiftly sail to war. This angered Agamemnon's wife, Clytemnestra, who began to plot his murder with the help of her lover, Aegisthus. They have waited for him to return for ten years and finally, when the play opens, they have their chance. As Agamemnon discovers their affair, Clytemnestra and Aegisthus kill him. Agamemnon's son, Orestes, and his other daughter, Elektra, want revenge for their father's death. Elektra convinces Orestes to murder their mother and Aegisthus. He complies, even though he knows that certain punishment awaits him.

The Furies consider matricide, or murder of a mother, to be the highest offense. Tisiphone (avenger of murder), Megaera (the jealous), and Alecto (constant anger) relentlessly hunt Orestes all the way to Athens. They vow to follow and haunt him without mercy for his crimes for eternity. Orestes seeks the help of the gods to persuade the Furies that he had the right to murder Clytemnestra. The god Apollo and the goddess Athena answer his pleas. Apollo volunteers to represent Orestes in court against the Furies, and Athena presides as judge. Just when it seems that Orestes will be found guilty, Athena rules him innocent. Orestes is then freed from the wrath of the Furies, who are forced to retreat and leave him in peace. The trial of Orestes is considered to be the first trial by jury.

Orestes Pursued by the Furies
by William-Adolphe Bouguereau

In *The Abduction of Proserpine,* by Dutch painter Rembrandt Harmenszoon van Rijn (1631), a protesting Persephone is dragged away by Hades, who shows careless disregard for his deed.

HADES

CHAPTER 3

A Queen for Hades

When Hades went to Zeus for advice about who should be his queen, Zeus offered Persephone (pur-SEF-uh-nee), his daughter with Demeter. Hades was thrilled—but no one told Persephone or Demeter of the arrangement.

After his talk with Zeus, Hades climbed into his chariot, drawn by four coal-black horses. Wearing his helmet of invisibility, he sped up through layers of rock and soil to the earth's surface. After riding around the earth for hours, looking for his promised bride, he finally found her picking wildflowers in a grassy field. Demeter was also gathering blossoms some distance away.

As Persephone filled her basket with lilies and violets, she wandered far from her mother. Inside a cool, moist wood, she spied the red petals of a poppy. She thought, "Mother would love that beautiful flower."

Persephone called out to Demeter, but Demeter was too far away to hear her. Not wanting to lose an opportunity to surprise her beloved mother, Persephone hurried over to pick the poppies.

Just then, the earth rumbled in a strange way. Persephone had heard earthquakes caused by Poseidon, but this was different. When the rumbling stopped, Hades stood before her.

Persephone had never seen Hades, but she knew who he was. His shadowy, forbidding appearance fit the description she had heard from her mother. Persephone's skin crawled as she looked at him. The way he watched her made her shiver.

Hades held a helmet in his hands. Persephone looked at it, then back at his face. In that instant, she knew what Hades had come for. She ran toward her mother, calling for help.

Hades ran to his chariot and whipped his horses into a frenzy, driving them toward Persephone. When he snatched her off her feet, Persephone gasped. He plopped his prize in the chariot beside him, causing her to drop the poppies she had picked for Demeter.

Wide-eyed with fear, Persephone peered over the edge of the chariot. They were going so fast, the wind made her eyes water. When Hades shouted and the earth yawned before them, Persephone's breath caught in her throat. As they rode into the wide chasm and the ground closed over them, the girl held on to the chariot for dear life.

About that time, Demeter looked around for Persephone in the field of flowers. "Persephone! Persephone! Where are you?" she called.

Persephone didn't answer. Demeter looked in the fields of pansies, violets, and daisies. She looked in fields of clover, wheat, and barley, calling Persephone's name wherever she went. There was no reply. For nine days she searched for Persephone, but found no sign of her.

On the tenth day Hecate (HEH-kah-tee), goddess of the moon, came to Demeter. "I have heard you shout Persephone's name," she said to the distraught mother. "Let us go to Helios, god of the Sun, to see if he knows anything about your daughter."

Helios listened to the story of Persephone's disappearance. With tears in her eyes, Demeter asked, "Do you know where my daughter is?"

Helios nodded. "She is with Hades. Zeus, her father, gave him permission to take Persephone as his wife. Now she is queen of the Underworld."

Demeter's heart sank. No mother wanted her daughter to live in such a dark, dismal place. Demeter screamed her rage and shook a fist at Mount Olympus.

At first she was so angry she wanted to do something—anything!—to get Persephone back. But then her anger turned to sadness.

She sank down to the ground, crying bitter tears. She forgot about her responsibilities as she cried for her daughter.

Demeter's tears moistened the ground around her, but that was the only water on the earth for many months. In her grief, Demeter neglected to send rain. Trees and flowers shriveled. Farmers tried to plant crops, but the dry, hard ground prevented the seeds from sprouting. Without grain, fruits, and vegetables, people became hungry. Without flower blossoms, the bees had no pollen to make honey. The gods ran out of ambrosia.

The famine lasted a year. When Zeus saw how bleak everything looked, he sent Hermes to convince Demeter to make things grow again.

Demeter refused. "I will end the famine when my daughter is back with me," she said.

Zeus knew the famine was his fault. He told Hermes to go to Hades and bring Persephone back to earth. With his winged sandals, the messenger god flew off.

Three-headed Cerberus wagged his tail in greeting when he saw Hermes.[1] Through the gates to the Underworld, Hermes proceeded to the thrones of Hades and his queen. He greeted them with a bow. "My lord and lady," he said, "your brother Zeus requests that you return Persephone to her mother without haste."

Persephone was excited at the thought of returning to her home and mother. But Hades was smart. He thought of a way to trick Persephone into staying with him. "Please eat a pomegranate seed before you leave," he urged her. "It will help you on your journey home." Persephone agreed and ate the juicy seed. (Another myth said Hades did not trick Persephone; instead, she ate seven pomegranate seeds from a bush while taking a walk.[2])

Before Hermes left Olympus, Demeter and Zeus had agreed that if Persephone had not eaten anything in Hades, she could return home.[3] When Demeter discovered Persephone had eaten the fruit, she cried out in anger and grief.

Return of Persephone, an 1891 painting by Lord Frederic Leighton, shows Hermes conducting Persephone to a happy reunion with Demeter.

Zeus agreed to a compromise. Because she had eaten the fruit, she would dwell with Hades for part of the year. For the rest of the year, she could live with her mother on Earth.

Each time Persephone left for Hades, Demeter refused to send rain. This caused the crops to stop growing. When Persephone returned to her mother at the end of her time with Hades, Demeter caused everything to flower again. According to the Greeks, this story about Persephone and Demeter explained the changing of the seasons.[4]

Persephone's Revenge

Persephone by
Dante Gabriel Rossetti

Hades was not happy. After forcing Persephone to leave her home and marry him, he had not found marriage to be all that he had hoped. He longed to be loved. But Persephone, who had been ordered by Zeus to live in Hades for six months of the year, refused to gracefully accept her lot in life. She pouted daily on her throne. Everyone in the kingdom witnessed how she cried constantly and railed at her husband about her unhappiness.

Hades despaired of ever seeing Persephone smile. Every day he offered her precious jewels from the bowels of the Earth. But Persephone continued to reject him. Hades realized he would have to look for love elsewhere.

Hades found it with a nymph from the Cocytus River. Her name was Menthe (MEN-thee). When they first met, the nymph seemed friendly and responded to Hades' attempts to converse. Soon, they were in love.

The god of the Underworld rarely left his domain, but as he secretly made more and more visits to Earth to visit Menthe, Persephone became suspicious. She decided to follow him.

When Persephone saw Hades greet Menthe and the couple embraced, she was shocked. She loathed the sight of her husband, but she was angry that he had betrayed her. Later, when Hades returned to his kingdom, Persephone pounced on Menthe, trampling the nymph to death.

The next day when Hades went to meet his lover, his calls to her were met with silence. As he approached their rendezvous location, he found her battered and bruised body on the ground. Somebody had beaten her to death! Hades' ire grew as he realized what had happened. Persephone didn't want him, but she didn't want anyone else to have him either.

Hades grieved for his lost love. Wanting to do something to honor Menthe's memory, he transformed her into a beautiful and fragrant plant called mint.[5]

While most myths say that Persephone was responsible for Menthe's death, one says her mother, Demeter, turned Menthe to dust.[6]

Sisyphus, by the 16th-century Italian artist Tiziano Vecellio (also referred to as Titian), shows Sisyphus carrying his boulder up the hill. The myths say he pushed the rock instead.

HADES

CHAPTER 4

Great Escapes

Although Hades adhered to strict rules about who could come or go from the Underworld, sometimes mortals came in uninvited or left by trickery. They usually suffered for it.

One mortal who escaped from Hades and lived to regret it was Sisyphus (SIH-suh-fus). Sisyphus lived in the city of Corinth with his wife, Merope (MEH-ruh-pee). Knowing that he and Merope would be separated at death, Sisyphus thought of a plan to outsmart Hades.

In the Greek tradition, the loved ones of someone who has died hold a funeral and dress in black to show their grief. On the day that Sisyphus' last breath left his body, Merope threw his corpse behind a rock and put on a red dress. She did not put a coin under his tongue. "I'm glad he's gone," she told her friends. "Let's celebrate!"

The soul of Sisyphus traveled to Hades. Since Sisyphus had no coin, Charon refused him passage across the Styx.

Stranded on the edge of the dark river, Sisyphus cried to Hades and Persephone, who were seated on their thrones. "My wife has neglected me in my death!" he complained.

"Merope shall be punished!" Hades told him.

"A proper punishment would be if you sent me back to torment her," Sisyphus said.

"You may return to Merope and teach her to respect the dead," agreed Hades. "Then return here."

When he walked through the door of their home, Merope hugged him. "We did it!" she cried. "We tricked Hades!"

Months passed. Hades searched for Sisyphus, but it was as if the mortal and his wife had vanished. Hades' only clues came from other gods who had spotted Sisyphus.

"He swam among the whales last winter," said Poseidon, the god of the sea.

"I saw him trading for baskets in the marketplace of the village last summer," said Hestia.

"Sisyphus picked barley from my fields at harvest," said Demeter.

When Hades realized he had been tricked, he bided his time.

Years later, Sisyphus' mortal body again died. He used a coin to cross the Styx. When Sisyphus walked into Hades' palace, the king greeted him. "Sisyphus, I know you miss Merope. Push this boulder to the top of that hill and you may return to your wife."

The rock stood taller than Sisyphus and weighed many tons. Sisyphus pushed against the boulder, straining with every part of his being. The rock moved an inch.

Years passed. Sisyphus shoved at the boulder daily. The closer he got to the top of the hill, the faster his heart raced. "Soon I should see my beloved wife's face!" he thought.

In his excitement, Sisyphus' hands became clammy. On his next push the rock slipped and fell to the bottom of the hill. Sisyphus had to begin again. The Greeks believed that those who journeyed to Hades would see Sisyphus pushing the boulder. And pushing. And pushing.[1]

Another mortal—Tantalus—suffered one of the most severe punishments in Hades. Tantalus was the son of Zeus and Pluto (whose name means "wealth" but was not the same as Hades). Because Pluto was a god of wealth, Tantalus was rich and famous throughout Asia and Greece.

His parents were respected gods, so Tantalus was permitted to dine at Zeus's table and listen to talk among the immortals. He became jealous of their powers and began to pester the gods. He

Punishment of Tantalus, by Gioacchino Assereto, a 17th-century Italian artist,
illustrates the agony of a soul caught in torment in the bowels of the Underworld.

betrayed their secrets. Then he stole their precious nectar and ambrosia from Mount Olympus and gave it to his friends on Earth. He also hid a gold statue of a dog that came from Zeus' temple in Crete. When Zeus demanded it back, Tantalus swore he had never seen it and did not return it.

His worst deed was when he invited the gods to his palace for dinner and served them stew made with human flesh. When the other gods saw what had been put before them, they were disgusted and furious. They threw Tantalus down to Tartarus. There he was punished for eternity with several torments.

Tantalus had to stand in the middle of a lake whose waters came to his chin. Soon, he became thirsty. When he bent to take a drink, the water went down. Dark, dry earth lay at his feet.

Tantalus suffered a similar punishment with hunger. Beautiful fruit trees grew on the edges of the lake in which he stood. Looking up, he saw arched boughs hanging over his head. The branches hung heavy with juicy pears, red apples, glowing pomegranates, plump figs, and green olives. Tantalus closed his eyes and licked his dry lips. He could imagine how sweet and juicy those fruits would taste to his parched throat and empty stomach.

But the moment he reached to pluck the fruit, a strong wind whipped the branches into the clouds. Not just once or twice did the branches stretch out of Tantalus' reach, but every time he reached overhead.

Tantalus' last and most terrible torment was his fear of death. A great block of stone hung in the air over his head and constantly threatened to crush him.[2]

One mortal who received Hades' blessing was Protesilaus (proh-TEH-seh-lous). He was the first Greek soldier to die in the Trojan War. After his death, his devoted wife begged Hades to allow her husband to return to life for three hours. Her prayer was answered, but when he died the second time, she killed herself so that she could follow her husband.[3]

Ixion and Tityus

Sisyphus and Tantalus were part of a quartet of infamous criminals who earned the label the Four Sinners. Their misdeeds earned them the worst torments in Hades. Ixion and Tityus rounded out the group.

Ixion, an evil king from Thessaly, was the first mortal to kill another person. When Ixion married Dia, he told his father-in-law, Deioneus, that he had some gifts for him. When he arrived, Ixion killed him, then went mad for what he had done. The only one who would purify Ixion and restore his sanity was Zeus.

In *Ixion* by José Ribera, Ixion is chained to a wheel.

After he was well, Ixion attacked Hera, the queen of Olympus. When Hera told Zeus what Ixion had done, Zeus set a trap for the man. He created a cloud in Hera's likeness. When Zeus witnessed Ixion trying to grab the cloud, thinking it was Hera, Zeus captured him and sent him to Tartarus. There, Ixion was strapped to a wheel. (In some myths the wheel was on fire. In others, it carried snakes.) The monotonous wheel whirled constantly and would continue to do so for eternity, with Ixion attached to its spokes.[4]

Tityus committed a similar offense when he attacked the goddess Leto. This mother asked two of her children, the gods Apollo and Artemis, to repay Tityus for his actions. They did so by stretching his body over several acres in Hades. Two vultures, always hunched on either side of him, continuously dug into his liver. Tityus was powerless to chase them off, and his liver continued to grow back forever.[5]

Heracles, Theseus, and Peirithous in the Underworld, carved in stone. Most of those who ventured into Hades' realm were not allowed to leave.

HADES

CHAPTER 5

Heroes in Hades

While some souls tried to leave Hades once they had arrived, others dared to enter before their time. They were hard pressed to find their way out again. Some of them never made it.

One day, King Peirithous (PEER-ih-thoos) came to see his friend, King Theseus (THEE-see-us). "I am in love with a beautiful woman," he said. "Will you help me bring her to my castle so that we can marry?"

"Of course!" said Theseus. "I am the bravest man alive. I have conquered the Amazons, a fierce race of fighting women from Asia. I have killed the Minotaur, a monster that was half-bull, half-man. Who is this woman?"

"Persephone, Demeter's daughter," Peirithous said.

Theseus' eyes widened. "Persephone is married to Hades!"

"She hates Hades and wants out of that gloomy place."

Theseus agreed to go, and the two buckled on their swords. They descended to Tartarus, deep in the heart of Hades, by the side entrance near Lake Avernus in Italy. (Other entrances to the Underworld were said to be through caves containing hot springs located at Plutonia, Taenarum in Laconia, and at Heraclea on the Euxine Sea.[1])

Peirithous and Theseus edged around Cerberus and approached Hades, seated on his throne. Hades scowled at the strangers. "Who are you and what do you want?" he roared.

Theseus introduced Peirithous and himself, then said, "We believe Persephone is unhappy here. We want to rescue her from this place so that my friend can marry her."

Hades scratched his chin. "Let's talk. Have a seat on my comfortable bench."

Theseus and Peirithous plopped on the seat. Immediately, they realized it was no ordinary piece of wood as it grabbed them and held them tightly.

Hades roared, "You poor fools will stay here forever!"[2]

Hades might have thought he could keep the two mortals captive, but another adventurer changed those plans. Heracles (HAYR-uh-kleez), known as Hercules (HER-kyoo-leez) to the Romans, was a great hero. He had accepted a challenge from an earthly king, Eurystheus, to complete twelve nearly impossible tasks. His final task was to remove the ferocious Cerberus from Hades and take it to Eurystheus.

As he passed through the gates of Hades, Heracles saw Theseus and Peirithous imprisoned. He managed to free Theseus but not Peirithous.

During his time in the Underworld, Heracles also wounded Hades—he accidentally shot him with a poisoned arrow. Hades had to travel to Olympus to see Paeon, the god of healing.[3]

After talking with many shades (spirits) in the Underworld, Heracles sacrificed one of Hades' cows. When the herdsman, Menoetes, saw what had happened, he challenged Heracles to a fight. Heracles seized him around the waist and broke his ribs, but he let him go when Persephone intervened.[4]

Heracles then asked Hades for Cerberus. Hades said he could borrow him if he could overpower the beast using no weapons.[5] Despite the animal's frightening appearance, Heracles grasped the beast and didn't loosen his grip until the beast quit fighting. He took Cerberus to show Eurystheus, and afterward returned the hellhound to Hades.[6]

For his help in rescuing Theseus and his other heroic accomplishments, Heracles was made immortal. He was given a home on Mount Olympus and the goddess Hebe for a wife.[7]

HERCVLES CERBERVM TRICIPITEM AD SVPEROS PERTRAXIT ·

Hercules Capturing Cerberus, an illustration by Hans Sebald Beham, from *The Labours of Hercules*, published in 1548. The fires of the Underworld blaze around the hero as he tries to capture the hound.

Another mortal who visited the Underworld was Aeneas. This Trojan hero was destined to build a mighty city. The problem was, he did not know where it should be located. Every place he tried, omens let him know he had chosen the wrong location.

Aeneas sought the advice of his deceased father, Anchises, in the Underworld. Aeneas believed his father would guide him to the elusive land.

Along the way to Hades, Aeneas met the Sibyl of Cumae, a prophetess who told him of the secret passage from Earth to Hades near Lake Avernus. She said his journey would be tricky. "Easy is the descent to Hades: night and day the door stands open," she warned, "but to recall the steps and pass out to the upper air, this is the task, this the toil!"[8]

She told Aeneas to carry a golden bough that would serve as his ticket into Hades. Aeneas didn't know how a golden branch would help him enter the Underworld, but he did as she said.

As Aeneas and the Sibyl approached Charon, the ferryman saw Aeneas without a coin. He refused to bring the boat to the shore—then Charon spied the golden bough. He allowed Aeneas and the wise woman to enter his boat without payment.

Cerberus started to growl upon seeing the couple, but when the Sibyl offered the beast a piece of bread with poppy seeds, he ate it. Because of the sleep-inducing properties of the poppies, Cerberus promptly fell asleep.

In the Underworld, Aeneas and the Sibyl saw three judges who told dead souls where they must spend their time. They also saw Dido, Aeneas' lover who chose to die rather than to live without him. Aeneas loved her, but Hermes, the messenger god, had reminded him of his destiny and told him he must continue on his journey. When he left Dido to do the gods' bidding, she felt betrayed, and she ignored him when she saw him in the Underworld.

Aeneas and the Sibyl also heard the groans from souls punished for evil deeds. Hurrying past these depressing scenes, they found Aeneas' father in the Elysian Fields.

Aeneas and Anchises greeted each other with hugs and tears. When Aeneas asked his father for help in finding his kingdom, Anchises told him he should settle in Italy. "Live there and you will prosper," Anchises said. He also advised Aeneas of how to avoid and to endure the hardships that lay before him. Then he led Aeneas to Lethe, the river of forgetfulness. After drinking from it, Aeneas would forget his time in the place of the dead, but he would remember his father's advice.

Aeneas and Anchises said good-bye. Aeneas was not sad. He knew he would see his father again. He returned to Earth with the Sibyl and sailed up the coast of Italy, looking for his promised home.[9]

Aeneas with the Sibyl and Charon, by Guiseppe Maria Crespi, shows the Sibyl of Cumae holding the golden bough, which would grant her and Aeneas passage with Charon and entrance to the Underworld.

Theseus, Heracles, and Aeneas may have been able to leave Hades, but most mortals were not as lucky.

Orpheus (OR-fee-us) loved the wood nymph Eurydice (yoo-RIH-dih-kee). Just after he and Eurydice were married, a serpent bit Eurydice and she died. Her spirit went to the Underworld.

Aeneas and Anchises in Hades, by French painter Alexandre Ubeleski, shows the idyllic setting of the Elysian Fields, where Aeneas met his father in the Underworld.

Orpheus begged Zeus to allow him to go to Hades to find his beloved wife and bring her back to Earth. Zeus knew few living mortals were allowed to leave the dark realm of Hades. He didn't want to lose Orpheus, who played beautiful music on a seven-stringed lyre, but he agreed to let Orpheus go.

When Orpheus saw gruff Charon, the boatman, at the lakeshore, he played his lyre and Charon ferried him across at no charge. When Cerberus saw Orpheus approaching the entrance to Hades, all of the dogs' heads began barking. The noise was deafening!

Orpheus again began to play his lyre. On earth, his relaxing music caused the trees to dance and the wild beasts to lie down in the field. In the Underworld, Cerberus stopped barking and closed

his eyes. All the souls listened and wept. Even Tantalus, Tityus, Sisyphus, and Ixion were soothed. The evil Furies cried for joy.

Orpheus approached Persephone and Hades sitting on their royal thrones and told them of his deep love for Eurydice. "Please allow me to take her back with me on Earth," he pleaded. "My life means nothing without her."

Hades said, "You and Eurydice may leave, Orpheus, but you must promise not to look back at your beloved's face on your way out. If you do, she will stay here forever."

As he and Eurydice set off toward Earth's surface, Orpheus' thoughts tumbled over each other in excitement. Soon his beloved

Orpheus Leading Eurydice from the Underworld by Jean-Baptiste-Camille Corot (1861). Soothed by his music, the shades of the dead watch as Orpheus tries to bring his beloved wife back to life.

would be back in his arms! Her lovely face would not be just in his dreams, but close to his own. In his excitement and fear that she was not actually behind him, he turned to gaze at his wife.

For a moment Eurydice's face was before him. Then, to his horror, it faded from view as though through a fog.

Orpheus groaned, knowing he would never see Eurydice alive again. In his despair, he played his lyre, but the song was so sad, his heart quit beating. (Another myth tells a different story about how he died—that a group of wild women called Manaeds attacked and killed him.[10])

When the gods saw what had become of Orpheus, they placed his lyre in the heavens as the bright constellation Lyra, where it would always remind them of Orpheus' great love for Eurydice.

The stories of Hades are as shadowy as the region in which the Greeks said he lived. Although the subject of Hades is usually not a popular one, the idea of a place for souls to go after death is established in most cultures and religions throughout the world.

Although the location of Hades kept changing as Greek culture evolved, the personality of the monarch of the Underworld was more stable. Hades ruled his kingdom fairly, though his temperament surpassed his reputation. He was respected and revered by those who cared for the condition of the departed. However, mortals also feared him. Because it was nearly impossible to sway his judgment, few temples were built in his honor. Hades was rarely shown in art.

Still, Hades' stories are full of love, jealousy, travels, heroes, beauty, and justice. Upon reading them, we see a distinctly different character from any other in Greek mythology. The king of the Underworld may not have been the mightiest Greek god, but he made his presence known among the others in steady fashion.

Hades in Later Religions

As religious beliefs changed from the polytheistic view of the ancient Greeks and Romans to the monotheistic view of Judaism, Christianity, and other modern religions, traces of the old mythologies remain and are acknowledged in modern sacred texts. The Bible uses the Greek word *Hades* when it talks about the place where sinners are sent. The Hebrew phrase "You will not abandon my soul to Hades" (Acts 2:27) shows that Christians believed Hades was not a place where a purified soul would go after death. Christians believed purified souls went to Heaven.

The words of Matthew 11:23 show Hades to be in a different location than the Christian Heaven. "And you, Capernaum [a town on the shore of the Sea of Galilee], will not be exalted to heaven, will you? You will descend to Hades."

The word *Hades* appears in Jesus' promise to Peter in Matthew 16:18: "Upon this rock I will build my church and the gates of Hades should not prevail against it."

The Old Testament of the Bible also uses the word *Sheol* when talking about the Underworld. *Sheol* was similar to the Greeks' Hades. It was below the surface of the earth (Ezekiel 31:15, 17; Psalm 86:13); a place of darkness (Job 10:21) and silence (Psalm 94:17) and forgetfulness (Psalm 88:12).

While the ancient Greeks believed Hades ruled the Underworld, Christians and Jews believed one God was the ruler of Sheol, Heaven, and Earth. Satan was seen as the antithesis to God, ruler of the Underworld.

Adherents to the Hindu religion believe a judgment awaits all beings in the next world, according to their conduct in this world. They also believe the gods were merely mortals until they bought immortality from the Supreme Being by sacrifices. In one translation of the Satapatha Brahmana, a Hindu sacred text, the Ruler of the Underworld is referred to as the "Ender."[11]

The Islamic culture believes Muhammad, the founder, had a vision in which he visited the heavens and saw the fires of Hell. He also visited the levels of heaven guarded by different biblical prophets.[12]

Chapter 1. Battle of the Titans

1. Francois Lenormant, *The Beginnings of History* (New York: Charles Scribner's Sons, 1891), p. 361.
2. Donald Richardson, *Great Zeus and All His Children* (Englewood Cliffs, NJ: Prentice-Hall, 1984), p. 10.
3. Dante Alighieri, *The Divine Comedy: Volume 1, Inferno*, translated by Mark Musa (New York: Penguin Books, 2003), lines 17–20.
4. Hesiod, *Theogony*, translated by Dorothea Wender (New York: Penguin Books, 1973), lines 737–741.
5. H.A. Guerber, *The Myths of Greece and Rome* (New York: British Book Center, Inc., 1963), p. 95.
6. Jenny March, *Cassell's Dictionary of Classical Mythology* (New York: Sterling Publishing Company, Inc., 1998), pp. 322–323.
7. Robert Graves, *Greek Gods and Heroes* (New York: Dell Publishing, 1960), p. 20.
8. Homer, *The Odyssey*, translated by Robert Fagles (New York: Penguin Books, 1996), Book 11, lines 582–592.
9. March, p. 341.
10. Virgil, *Aeneid*, translated by Charles E. Bennett (New York: Allyn & Bacon, 1904), Book 7, line 383.
11. Baron George L. Lyttelton, *Dialogues of the Dead*, translated by Elizabeth Robinson (London: W. Sandby, 1860), p. 209.
12. March, p. 640.
13. Dante, Canto VIII.68.

Chapter 2. Hades' Hospitality

1. Dante Alighieri, *The Divine Comedy: Volume 1, Inferno*, translated by Mark Musa (New York: Penguin Books, 2003), lines 82–89.
2. Jenny March, *Cassell's Dictionary of Classical Mythology* (New York: Sterling Publishing Company, Inc., 1998), p. 202.
3. Edith Hamilton, *Mythology* (Boston: Little, Brown and Co., 1942), p. 43.
4. H.A. Guerber, *The Myths of Greece and Rome* (New York: London House & Maxwell, 1907), p. 96.
5. John Milton, *Paradise Lost*, translated by Arthur Wilson Verity (London: Cambridge University Press, 1907), Book 2, line 583.
6. Hesiod, *Theogony and Works and Days*, translated by Dorothea Wender (New York: Penguin Books, 1973), lines 310–312.
7. Hesoid, *Theogony*, lines 769–774.
8. Robert Graves, *Greek Gods and Heroes* (New York: Dell Publishing, 1960), p. 31.
9. Homer, *Iliad*, translated by Robert Fagles (New York: Penguin Books, 1990), Book 8, line 10.
10. Hesoid, *Theogony,* lines 821–822.
11. Ibid., line 297.
12. Ibid., lines 853–869.
13. Ibid., lines 148–154.
14. Edith Hamilton, *Mythology* (Boston: Little, Brown and Company, 1969), p. 44.
15. Aeschylus, *The Eumenides*, translated by Arthur Woollgar Verrall (London: Macmillan and Co., 1908), pp. 13–15.
16. Hamilton, pp. 415–417.
17. Homer, *The Odyssey*, translated by Robert Fagles (New York: Penguin Books, 1996), Book 4, lines 635–639.
18. Hesiod, *Works and Days*, lines 170–174.
19. Aeschylus, lines 46–59.

Chapter 3. A Queen for Hades

1. Hesiod, *Theogony and Works and Days*, translated by Dorothea Wender (New York: Penguin Books, 1973), line 769–774.
2. Ovid, *The Metamorphoses*, translated by Horace Gregory (New York: New American Library, 2001), Book 5, line 538.
3. Apollodorus, *The Library*, translated by Robin Hard (New York: Oxford University Press, 1997), 1.4.5–5.1.
4. Edith Hamilton, *Mythology* (Boston: Little, Brown and Company, 1969), p. 63.
5. Ovid, Book 10, line 728.
6. Patricia Turner, "Menthe," *Dictionary of Ancient Deities* (Jefferson, NC: McFarland and Co., 2000), p. 318.

Chapter 4. Great Escapes

1. Robert Graves, *Greek Gods and Heroes* (New York: Dell Publishing, 1960), pp. 59–61.
2. Gustav Schwab, *Gods and Heroes: Myths and Epics of Ancient Greece* (New York: Pantheon Books, 1946), pp. 147–148.
3. Virgil, *Aeneid*, translated by Charles E. Bennett (New York: Allyn & Bacon, 1904), p. 340, line 447.
4. Apollodorus, *The Library*, translated by Robin Hard (New York: Oxford University Press, 1997), 1.20.8.
5. Pindar, *The Olympian and Pythian Odes of Pindar*, translated by F.D.

Morice (London: Henry S. King & Co, 1876), Book 2, lines 20–22.

Chapter 5. Heroes in Hades

1. Henry Fanshawe Tozer, *Classical Geography* (London: Macmillan, 1887), p. 105, online at http://www.archive.org/details/classicalgeograp00tozeuoft; and "Earls of Plymouth," http://www.1911encyclopedia.org/Earls_of_Plymouth
2. H.A. Guerber, *The Myths of Greece and Rome* (New York: British Book Center, Inc., 1963), p. 275.
3. Apollodorus, *The Library*, translated by Robin Hard, (New York: Oxford University Press, 1997), 2.7.7.
4. Ibid., 2.5.12–6.2.8.
5. Ibid.
6. Ibid., 2.7.3.
7. Homer, *The Odyssey*, translated by Robert Fagles (New York: Penguin Books, 1996), Book 11, line 693.
8. Virgil, *Aeneid*, translated by Charles E. Bennett (New York: Allyn & Bacon, 1904), Book 6, line 126.
9. Edith Hamilton, *Mythology* (Boston: Little, Brown and Company, 1969), pp. 320–334.
10. Apollodorus, 1.3.1–3.
11. Monier Williams, *Non-Christian Religious Systems: Hinduism* (New York: E. & J. B. Young & Co., 1885), p. 35.
12. Ibid., pp. 26–27.

Books

Davis, Kenneth C. *Don't Know Much About Mythology: Everything You Need to Know about the Greatest Stories in Human History But Never Learned*. New York: HarperCollins Publishers, 2005.

Nardo, Don. *Greek and Roman Mythology*. San Diego: Greenhaven Press, 2002.

Pearson, Anne. *Eyewitness Ancient Greece*. New York: DK Children, 2007.

Roberts, Russell. *How'd They Do That in Ancient Greece?* Hockessin, DE: Mitchell Lane Publishers, 2010.

Works Consulted

Aeschylus. *The Eumenides*. Translated by Arthur Woollgar Verrall. London: Macmillan and Co., 1908.

Apollodorus. *The Library*. Translated by Robin Hard. New York: Oxford University Press, 1976.

Dante Alighieri. *The Divine Comedy: Vol. 1, Inferno*. Translated by Mark Musa. New York: Penguin Books, 2003.

Graves, Robert. *Greek Gods and Heroes*. New York: Dell Publishing, 1960.

———. *The Greek Myths, Vol. I*. New York: Penguin Books, 1977.

Guerber, H.A. *The Myths of Greece and Rome*. New York: London House & Maxwell, 1963.

Hamilton, Edith. *Mythology*. Boston: Little, Brown and Company, 1969.

Hesiod. *Theogony and Works and Days*. Translated by Dorothea Wender. New York: Penguin Books, 1973.

Holy Bible, NIV and ISV.

Homer. *Iliad*. Translated by Robert Fagles. New York: Penguin Books, 1990.

Homer. *Odyssey*. Translated by Robert Fagles. New York: Penguin Books, 1996.

Lenormant, Francois. *The Beginnings of History*. New York: Charles Scribner's Sons, 1891.

Lyttelton, Baron George L. *Dialogues of the Dead*. Translated by Elizabeth Robinson. London: W. Sandby, 1860.

March, Jenny. *Cassell's Dictionary of Classical Mythology*. London: Cassell & Co., 2001.

Milton, John. *Paradise Lost*. Translated by Arthur Wilson Verity. London: Cambridge University Press, 1907.

Ovid. *The Metamorphoses*. Translated by Horace Gregory. New York: New American Library, 2001.

Pindar. *The Olympian and Pythian Odes of Pindar*. Translated by F.D. Morice. London: Henry S. King & Co., 1876.

Richardson, Donald. *Great Zeus and All His Children*. Englewood Cliffs, NJ: Prentice-Hall, Inc., 1984.

———. *Greek Mythology for Everyone: Legends of the Gods and Heroes*. New York: Avenel Books, 1989.

Schwab, Gustav. *Gods and Heroes: Myths and Epics of Ancient Greece*. New York: Pantheon Books, Inc., 1957.

Stapleton, Michael. *The Illustrated Dictionary of Greek and Roman Mythology*. New York: Peter Bedrick Books, 1986.

Tozer, Henry Fanshawe. *Classical Geography*. London: Macmillan, 1887.

Turner, Patricia. "Menthe," *Dictionary of Ancient Deities*. Jefferson, NC: McFarland and Co., 2000.

Virgil. *Aeneid*. Translated by Charles E. Bennett. New York: Allyn & Bacon, 1904.

Williams, Monier. *Non-Christian Religious Systems: Hinduism*. New York: E. & J. B. Young & Co., 1885.

On the Internet

Ancient Greek and Roman Gods for Kids: Hades
http://greece.mrdonn.org/greekgods/hades.html

Cerberus: Three-headed Guard Dog of Hades
http://www.theoi.com/Ther/KuonKerberos.html

Hades: Greek King of the Underworld, God of the Dead
http://www.theoi.com/Khthonios/Haides.html

Mythography: The Greek God Hades in Myth and Art
http://www.loggia.com/myth/hades.html

Perseus Project: Hercules' Twelfth Labor: Cerberus
http://www.perseus.tufts.edu/Herakles/cerberus.html

GLOSSARY

ambrosia (am-BROH-juh)—The gods' favorite food, thought to have been made with honey.

banish (BAN-ish)—To legally force (someone) to leave.

chalice (CHAA-lis)—A drinking cup or goblet.

ferment (FUR-ment)—Process by which an ingredient, such as sugar, breaks down to produce alcohol.

immortal (ih-MOR-tul)—Unable to die.

lyre (LYR)—Musical stringed instrument of ancient Greece.

mortal (MOR-tul)—A human who lives on Earth; any being that can die.

nectar (NEK-ter)—A sweet drink made of honey.

nymph (NIMF)—A beautiful mythical creature thought to live in the woods or in a body of water.

prophetess (PRAH-feh-tess)—A female being who can tell the future. (A male who can foretell events is a prophet.)

purified (PYOOR-ih-fyd)—Condition in which a soul is cleansed and made ready to enter Heaven or the Underworld.

ruse (ROOZ)—A trick.

Sheol (SHEE-ohl)—A name for the Underworld.

Sibyl (SIH-bul)—A priestess or prophetess in ancient Greece.